The Tournament

In the Outback of Central Australia, there was a contest to see who, of all the wildlife that existed there, had the most beautiful voice. The contest was open to all of the birds, mammals, amphibians, and reptiles. It was going to be judged by a panel of experts from the Aboriginal Tribe known as the Pintupi People.

The Pintupis had occupied this area for hundreds of years and

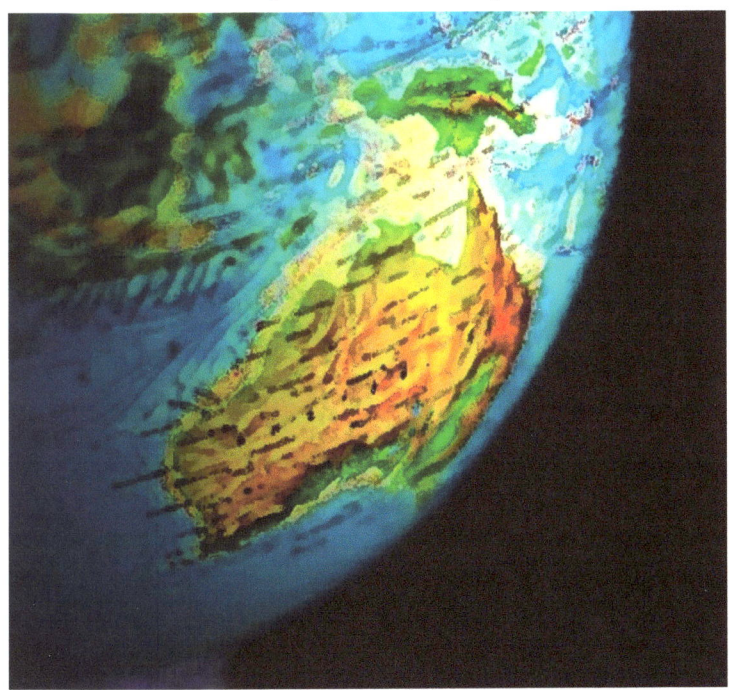

were known for their deep connection to nature. They loved being part of the animal world and enjoyed hosting various contests that honored many of their furry, feathery, and scaled friends.

All of the Outback's creatures were excited about participating in the upcoming singing contest. They could be heard honing their musical skills in the bushes, in the desert, and by the watering holes. The winner of this contest would be distinguished from all the rest by being given a special role in entertaining the entire community. This role was regarded with utmost respect. It was surely going to be one of the most competitive and exciting contests the Outback had ever seen.

The day of auditions arrived. The Pintupi People invited the mammals to be the first group to try out, as soon as the sun came up over the horizon. All of the mammals were anxiously waiting for their opportunity to demonstrate their voices.

Kangaroo, Wallaby, Koala, Dingo, and Camel made their way to the front of the line. Then Donkey, Water Buffalo, and others, including Opossum, soon followed. All of them were filled with anticipation at having a chance to shine their light. Only Bat trailed behind that day, finding it difficult to get out of his cave early in the morning and waking up with the sniffles to boot.

The Pintupis drew a sacred circle on the ground using little pebbles and invited each animal to step into the center. The judges listened to every participant and marked their scores using sticks in the sand. One tally mark meant they performed poorly, two tally marks meant they were adequate, but three tally marks in the sand meant they were exceptionally good and would move up to the next level in the contest. Once all of the scores for the mammals were tallied, the judges could then focus their attention on the next group.

Most of the mammals received two marks while several of them received three marks, and all were immediately placed on the Call Back

List for the following day. Only Bat, who was barely audible, received one mark and was politely asked to return home. He was told to take care of his cold before he infected others.

The second round of auditions was reserved for the amphibians and reptiles. Crocodile pushed his way to the front of the line, followed by Thorny Devil and Monitor Lizard. Then Tortoise, Scorpion, and Carpet Snake had their turns. Several others followed.

Last in line was Toad. He was hesitant to even audition that day. Toad had very little self-esteem to begin with, and he felt uneasy about what the others thought of his deep croaking voice. "Why bother?" he thought.

But Toad really wanted to participate in the Outback festivities with the others and decided to go anyway.

"Oh, well!" he said to himself. "I will give it a try."

The judges scored several of the contestants with two and three marks. Only Toad was given a one, and worse than that, he had to endure the heckling and teasing from many of the others. He sadly hopped away to hide by his favorite pond.

The third round of auditions was saved for the birds. Many Cacklers, Carolers, Trillers, Peepers, and Hooters eagerly flew in, bursting with anticipation to sing their most beautiful songs. Pelican, Brolga, and Emu were the largest ones, so they pressed their way through the crowd to be in the front of the line. Soon, Kiwi, Rainbow Lorikeet, Cuckoo, King Parrot, Cockatoo, and Laughing Kookaburra, to name just a few, took their spots.

Blackbird was the last to audition. She knew that nobody appreciated her fine whistle, yet she loved the music and wanted to support the contest just the same. Again, many of the birds were given three marks in the sand because so many of them had such magnificent voices. Others were given two marks and encouraged to try again the following year. Only Blackbird was given one mark, thanked for her time, and dismissed.

Squeak, Croak, Thrive!

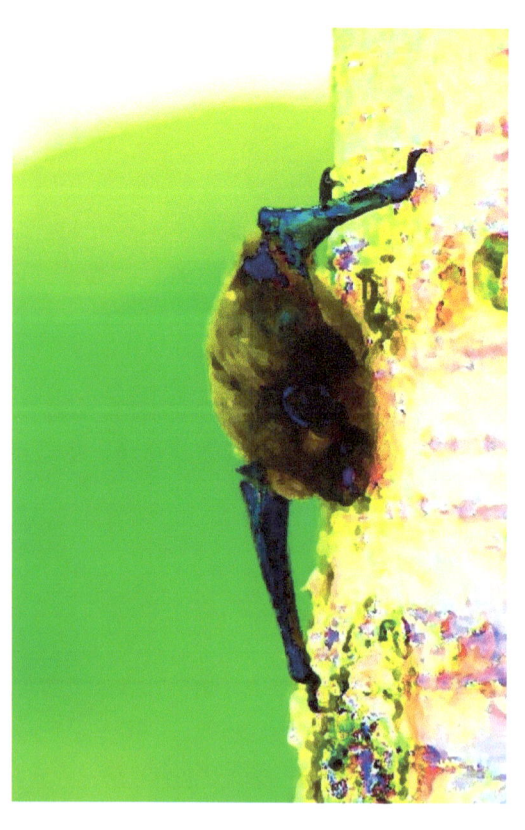

As Blackbird was flying back to her nest, she spotted Bat swooping in and out among some nearby trees. She thought she heard Bat sneeze.

"Bless you," said Blackbird in passing as she glided by.

"I wish someone would!" screeched Bat in a quiet voice. Blackbird stopped in mid-flight. She immediately flew down to Bat and asked, "Did you just say something?"

"Yes," Bat squeaked, "I said, I wish someone would bless me!"

Blackbird could barely make out

what Bat said, but she could tell that he was pretty upset. They found a thick branch on a nearby tree to perch upon.

"Do you want to talk about it?" inquired Blackbird. "I am a pretty good listener, you know."

Bat seemed to be taken by surprise. Nobody ever seemed to listen to him before. "Who was this Blackbird?" he wondered.

"Well, it's just that I wasn't feeling so good this morning," Bat replied. "Ahchoo!" He sneezed. "See, I woke up with a nasty cold today.

I didn't feel well enough to travel, but then I decided to audition for the Voice Contest anyway. Since they scheduled the contest for daylight, which is normally when I sleep, I was having trouble flying there. When I finally arrived, nobody even said hello to me. They just looked at me as if I was some sort of freak. There was so much dust and sand in the air, I just kept sneezing. Everyone moved away from me."

Bat put his head into his wing and sneezed again. "Even the judges! They weren't very nice either. This whole contest is rigged if you ask me."

"I see," said Blackbird, trying to be sympathetic. "It sounds like this hasn't been a very pleasant day for you, my friend. I'm sorry about that."

Just then, Toad came hopping by. He was croaking loudly.

"Hi Toad," said Blackbird. "How are you doing today?"

"Hmmm…. Don't ask!" Toad grumbled. "That contest is nothing but a fake! Those judges never even gave me a chance. They already knew who they liked, so why did they even bother having a contest? I don't need them anyway. Why should I waste my time croaking for them when none of them appreciates my talents?"

"I know exactly what you mean, Toad," screeched Bat. "They can have their stupid contest. We don't need them. We are better than any of them!"

"You can say that again," Toad agreed. "I'm sick of it! It makes me want to hide and never come out. That will show them!"

"Whoa, wait a minute," Blackbird interrupted. "Do you both hear yourselves? You are blaming everyone else and complaining about what happened to you. Where does that get you?"

Bat and Toad fell silent and stared at Blackbird.

"I thought the contest was great," said Blackbird. "I loved listening to all the performances! Everyone did their very best."

"Well," said Bat a bit sheepishly, "there were a lot of talented creatures auditioning today. I guess everyone did have something to offer." And then remembering how he was treated, he added "But we do too! And even if the judges didn't think we were the best, we are still talented in our own way! Maybe the loudest voice is not the most brilliant voice out there."

"You both know your own talents, it's just that others haven't recognized them yet," continued Blackbird.

"I know you both have something special to offer. I have something special to offer too. Guess what? Those judges rejected me just like they rejected you. They said my caw was weak and didn't carry as well as the other birds. So what! I'm not going to waste my time whining about it. I say we put our heads together and devise a plan that will show them how talented the three of us truly are. It doesn't do us any good complaining or getting angry. We need to do something about it! So, what do you say, fellas?"

Bat and Toad looked at one another and simultaneously cried, "Yea! Let's do it!" They both felt the passion in the words Blackbird had spoken. So, the three of them put their heads together to brainstorm a victory plan.

A Trip to the Hidden Cave

Blackbird knew of a cave in the darkest part of the forest where the moon never shines. She explained to her new friends that this cave was located near a mineral spring and was considered to have a powerful effect on anyone who visited there.

"I believe that if we travel to this far away cave, we might discover its hidden treasures and acquire some special qualities. Perhaps it will help us improve ourselves."

"You mean it might help me strengthen my voice?" asked Bat.

"Or help me raise my voice an octave or two?" croaked Toad.

"Who knows," Blackbird answered, "It could do wonders for all of us, even more than we ever dreamed of."

"I think we should start moving toward the cave now," Bat screeched, eager to get going.

"I agree," said Blackbird, "the sooner the better. However, we must travel without resting, for the moon will be full in just a couple of days. It is known that the best time to visit this cave is during the full moon. That is when we will experience the cave's greatest power. But we will have to travel both day and night to reach this place in time for miracles. Bat, would you be able to do that?"

A look of concern fell upon Bat's face. "I'm not sure. I always rest during the day, you know. I'm not exactly in the best shape after

spending a full day traveling to the contest, so I probably need more rest." Bat hung his head, "Maybe you should go without me."

"No, no! We should go together, just as we planned," said Blackbird.

"That's not a problem, Bat. I don't need much rest at all," Toad replied. "I can carry you on my back through the day, while you sleep. I'm strong."

"Great! That's the spirit, Toad," said Blackbird. "Besides, you will need your rest, Bat, because once we get to the cave, we are going to

have to rely upon you. You have the skills to navigate the cave's winding labyrinths, and only you can guide us through the darkness with your keen sight."

"Very well," Bat agreed, "but how we will find this mystical cave?"

Blackbird thought for a moment. "Well, I can fly ahead of you and navigate our path. I will communicate the directions back to you, so you can make your way by land." Then suddenly, Blackbird hesitated: "Uh-oh, there is one small problem. My voice is weak and doesn't carry that

far. Would you be able to hear me? " she asked with concern.

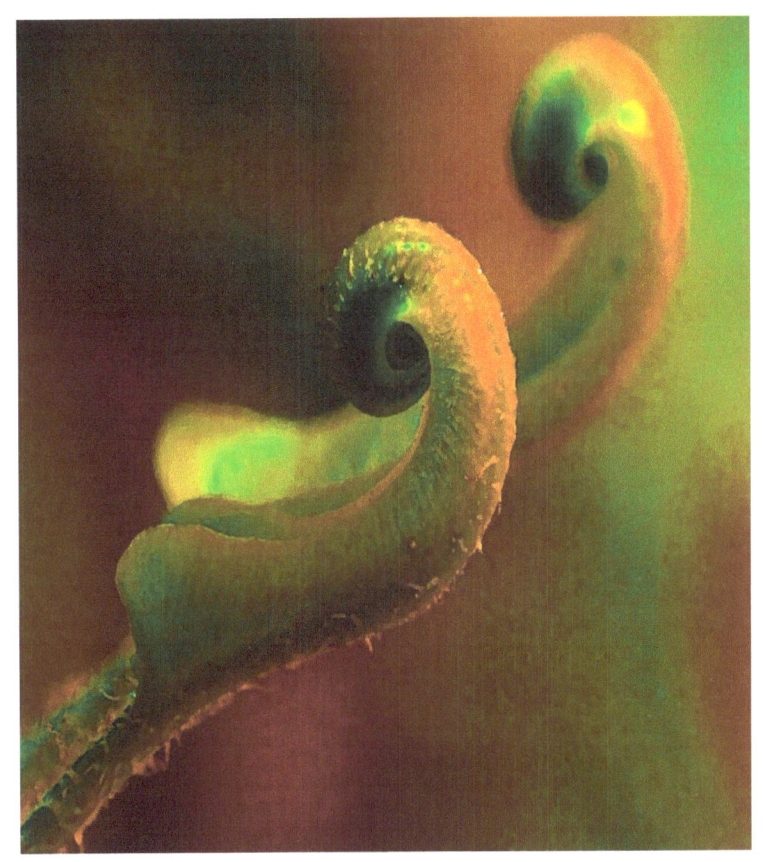

"No worries," Bat immediately responded. "I know a way to amplify your voice, Blackbird. We, bats, do it all of the time making megaphones out of big leaves.

You will need to fly to the top of a tree and choose the largest leaf that you can find. Then, curl up the leaf creating a smooth channel to amplify your voice. You will be surprised how much louder your voice will be."

Then Bat added: "Remember, I have exceptional hearing, so I will be sure to wake up when I hear your voice, even if I am sleeping on Toad's back. We will be able to navigate our way. Trust me."

"Incredible!" Blackbird trilled. "This is getting exciting! We should prepare to leave right away."

Just then, Toad began to panic. "Wait a minute," Toad shouted, "You both can fly. I am the one who has to stay on the ground. What if you both decide to fly to the cave and leave me in the dark forest alone? How will I be able to protect myself?"

Blackbird and Bat quickly came to Toad's side. "We would never do that to you, Toad! You are our friend," Blackbird said.

"Besides," Bat seconded, "You will be carrying me, remember? I need you just as much as you need me. So what do you say?"

Toad smiled big and croaked a resounding, "Yes!"

The three friends headed westward to begin their journey toward the magical cave in the forest where the moon never shines. They traveled through the barren desert all day, Blackbird flying overhead of Toad, who now carried the sleeping Bat. As the sun was setting, Bat began to awaken. He stretched out his folded wings and flew up to join Blackbird. He enjoyed flying beside her in the night sky. Toad continued to hop on the ground without missing a beat. They traveled this way until the sun peeked up over the horizon, and Bat started yawning. It was time for Bat and Blackbird to fly down to meet Toad.

"We covered a great distance in one day," Blackbird said. "Now, we should eat and get some rest. Let's look for food first and meet back

here in ten minutes, after we eat."

Blackbird flew to a nearby watering hole and feasted on worms. Toad found a few grubs and spiders to munch on. Bat was happy too, as he found a swarm of mosquitos to satisfy his appetite. Once they were all fed, they met up again to relax while they digested their food. After an hour or so, they were ready to resume their journey. Bat laid across Toad's back once again and immediately drifted off to sleep for the day. Blackbird flew up into the blue sky, and Toad hopped below her, carrying his load without any sign of strain.

In the Crystal Cave

After traveling for several hours, they came to a dense forest. Blackbird let out a loud caw and took off so quickly that Toad lost sight of her. Bat immediately woke up and tuned his ears to Blackbird.

Within minutes, Bat heard the amplified sound of Blackbird's voice. He jumped off Toad's back and screamed, "This way! We need to go this way!" With these words, Bat opened his wings and flew ahead, while Toad hopped tirelessly behind him on the ground.

The forest was so dense and so dark that Bat thought night had fallen. They continued to follow the sound of Blackbird for hours until at last, they came to what appeared to be a cave.

Bat could see it with his keen sense of sight. Toad was unable to see a thing in the darkness, but trusted his friend Bat, nonetheless. Just then, Blackbird swooped down to meet them. She had a cone shaped leaf in her beak.

"This is awesome, Bat! Thanks for the tip," Blackbird said, as she dropped the leaf to the ground. "I never would have imagined you could turn a leaf into a megaphone."

"I told you so," Bat said proudly. "Now, is this the mystical cave you spoke of?"

"I believe it is." Blackbird chirped. "Do you mind going inside and doing a bit of exploring for us?"

"Roger that!" Bat said, as he flew into the cave like a rocket on a mission. The others waited outside.

The forest was pitch black, so neither Blackbird nor Toad could see much of anything. They kept perfectly still and silent, staying close to one another for protection. Bat flew into the cave and navigated his way through a crystal cavern until he came upon an underground lake.

The water was cold and sweet as he bent down to taste it. Suddenly, he noticed something reflecting in the water. He looked up, and above his head, he saw stalactites and chains of little glow worms hanging from the ceiling. They looked like a myriad of twinkling stars. The cave exploded with light.

He rapidly flew back through the crystal caverns to return to his friends. "Wow! You have to see this!" Bat exclaimed with excitement. Quickly, Blackbird and Toad followed Bat into the cave. They were filled

with awe when they saw the glow worms shining brightly from the ceiling. They bent down and took a drink from the underground lake which Blackbird said held magical powers. The entire cave appeared to be magical. They rested under the glowing lights, basking in the beauty of the enchanted cave. Just then, Toad noticed an unusual looking crooked plant near the water. He hopped over to it for a closer look.

One of the sticks of the crooked plant had broken away from the others and was laying on its side. Toad noticed that the outside of the stick was hard to the touch, but the inside was soft and pliable.

Carefully, with his long finger, he pressed on the inner part and the

soft material came out leaving a hollow space inside. Toad pressed his mouth on one end of the stick and said, "I am Toad, I am Toad, I am Toad." The sound echoed through the cave like a mighty giant's voice.

All three friends began to laugh. Toad had found his own megaphone! They couldn't believe how powerful Toad's voice was when he spoke through the long stick which looked much like a didgeridoo. Toad had discovered an amazing instrument that could transform his current voice into one of majesty. The sound he was now making was rich, deep, and mystical.

"I want one too!" screeched Bat, unable to contain his excitement as he flew over to the crooked plant. Then, he noticed something round and shiny in the water. He flew down, nudged it out of the lake, and watched it roll on the ground. It was a beautiful, brown nautilus shell with a large opening on one side. Bat put his mouth on to the opening and said, "I am Bat, I am Bat, I am Bat!"

Bat's voice was not only loud, it was strong and clear. He played

around with it for a long time, listening to the variety of new frequencies it gave his once squeaky little voice.

"Now, we all have our own amplifiers," Bat stated happily. "Blackbird has her leaf, Toad has his didgeridoo, and I have my shell. We could form a band!" Bat exclaimed to the cave walls.

Suddenly, they all stopped and burst into laughter.

"A band?" cried out Toad.

"Yes, that's it! A trio," exclaimed Blackbird, and they began to chatter excitedly about the idea. They were eager to start sharing their stories and songs with the others who they had left behind in the Outback.

The Batty Trio

Now, more than anything, they also wanted to share their magical experience with everyone else. And why not? They all had something special to offer with their new amplified voices.

"We could practice here in the cave and improve our skills before

we announce our new band. Nobody would bother us here, and there's plenty to eat and drink," Bat said happily.

"Yes, and we could even come up with some ideas to encourage others to join us in singing! Maybe we can make some instruments to give the children to get them excited too. Then we can all make music!" Toad croaked loudly through his stick.

"Super cool!" shouted Bat.

"Awesome idea!" seconded Blackbird. "Hey, we could call ourselves The Batty Trio! After all, we are very resourceful and a bit wacky. Kids love that! We would make the perfect warm up band for the Clear Voice Contest every year. We can perform throughout the Outback and teach children and adults how to find ways to share their own talents."

"You mean we could be role models?" Bat excitedly asked. "I always hoped one day I could be a role model for someone!"

"Yes, we can travel throughout the Outback and teach children and adults how to find and share their talents!

The possibilities are truly limitless!" Blackbird said smiling.

"I can't wait to share the news with the others", beamed both Bat and Toad dreaming up their next adventure.

"But for now", Blackbird proposed, "let's practice!" And the three musicians picked up their amplifiers and began to sing.

They spent hours every day practicing their music. With every practice hour spent in the cave, their music became better and better, and their voices grew clearer and stronger. They also spent many hours exploring the cave, where they were able to find interesting things they could convert into other types of musical devices. They had loads of fun playing and testing things out.

Days went by really fast. It was time to return home. The journey back was a lot easier because they had so much to talk about.

When the trio arrived home, they were pleasantly surprised to

discover how happy the creatures of the Outback were to see them. Many of them said their sudden disappearance had caused much alarm. They feared the three friends had left the Outback for good. When the trio returned, everyone breathed a sigh of relief.

All the other creatures gathered around to listen to the story of the journey to the Crystal Cave and the discovery of the various voice amplifiers. It made the trio feel so good. They were treated like celebrities and everyone was anxious to hear them sing.

The following day, The Batty Trio made their way to the Pintupi Village with the treasures they brought back from the cave. The Pintupi People welcomed them and listened intently to the band's performance.

Everyone was especially impressed with how much Bat, Blackbird, and Toad had improved their voices, and how enthusiastic they were to help others.

The Pintupis agreed that The Batty Trio would make an excellent warm up band each year for the Voice Contest.

The judges also decided to create a special category called "Super Unique." Each year, the Pintupis would award some creature from the Outback a prize for the most unique talent.

The Batty Trio was invited to travel about the Outback and teach others to try new things and find their own talents. They felt honored with the invitation and happily agreed to promote the Voice Contest and generate excitement through their wonderful, participatory, musical style.

In time, Bat, Blackbird, and Toad became the most popular creatures in the Outback. But even more rewarding for our three friends was that they became role models for so many others.

Many animals, reptiles, amphibians, and birds came from far and wide to hear their enchanted, mystical sounds and empowering stories.

With much practice and love for their new career, The Batty Trio became an inspiration for everyone in all of Australia.

LEARN AND GROW WITH SACRED EARTH GUIDING TOTEMS

This book is one of the sixty-four Whimsical Tales from the Wild Heart. These nature stories are about magical journeys, struggles, and relationships of the 64 animal trios.

Our work is inspired by working with Dream Arc Totem Codex created by Richard Rudd (Gene Keys, UK).

Insects and underwater creatures represent our fears. Mammals symbolize longings, struggles, and accomplishments that they experience along the way. Birds signify a higher perspective of the journey and present a vision of the human potential. Together they form a global archetypal matrix of the most used and highly regarded totems of the planet.

Working with our 192 nature archetypes from different guidance systems will help you and your children see true magic in nature and establish closer relationship with wildlife and each other.

ABOUT THE AUTHORS

 **Paddy Lynn** is a professional storyteller, actress, author, and teacher with over thirty-five years of experience working with children. She combines her love for theatre and literature with her unique Storyacting programs, presenting over a hundred and fifty programs a year.

To learn about her educational programs for children and adults, or to book an event with her, visit http://paddylynn.com

 **Svetlana Pritzker** is the founder of New Human Energetics, a system that helps you overcome challenges and live on purpose. With over twenty five years of experience in education, she is highly passionate about helping parents and teachers raise inspired, creative, and empowered children.

Svetlana is an author of several books about co-creating relationships of love and trust and co-parenting motivated and capable children. To learn about her work or to book a personal session or an event, visit www.energy4action.com and www.youtube.com/Lanapritzker

ILLUSTRATIONS AND ACKNOWLEDGEMENTS

Svetlana and Yury Pritzker have been joyfully playing with colors and textures of photos, taken during their travels around the world, in order to share an enchantment and inspiration that they find in nature.

Special thanks

To Jon L. Lynn for his insight and thorough editing of totem stories

To the contributors of websites (below) for permission to use their royalty free photos as a base for crafting some of the illustrations for this book

http://www.sciencekids.co.nz

https://pixabay.com

www.ingramcontent.com/pod-product-compliance
Lightning Source LLC
Chambersburg PA
CBHW041536280526
45792CB00004B/1521